HAL•LEONARD INSTRUMENTAL PLAY-ALONG

CLARINET IN B♭

WEST SIDE STORY®

Based on a conception of Jerome Robbins

Book by
Arthur Laurents

Music by
Leonard Bernstein®

Lyrics by
Stephen Sondheim

Entire Original Production
Directed and Choreographed by
Jerome Robbins

ISBN 978-1-4234-5824-1

LEONARD BERNSTEIN Music Publishing Company LLC

BOOSEY & HAWKES

AN IMAGEM COMPANY

DISTRIBUTED BY
HAL•LEONARD® CORPORATION
7777 W. BLUEMOUND RD. P.O. BOX 13819 MILWAUKEE, WI 53213

Visit Hal Leonard Online at
www.halleonard.com

How To Use The CD Accompaniment:

A melody cue appears on the right channel only. If your CD player has a balance adjustment, you can adjust the volume of the melody by turning down the right channel.

The CD is playable on any CD player, and is also enhanced so PC and MAC users can adjust the recording to any tempo without changing the pitch.

AMERICA

CLARINET IN B♭

Lyrics by STEPHEN SONDHEIM
Music by LEONARD BERNSTEIN

2 COOL

CLARINET IN B♭

Lyrics by STEPHEN SONDHEIM
Music by LEONARD BERNSTEIN

❸ I FEEL PRETTY

CLARINET IN B♭

Lyrics by STEPHEN SONDHEIM
Music by LEONARD BERNSTEIN

4 I HAVE A LOVE

CLARINET IN B♭

Lyrics by STEPHEN SONDHEIM
Music by LEONARD BERNSTEIN

5 JET SONG

CLARINET IN B♭

Lyrics by STEPHEN SONDHEIM
Music by LEONARD BERNSTEIN

6 MARIA

CLARINET IN B♭

Lyrics by STEPHEN SONDHEIM
Music by LEONARD BERNSTEIN

7 ONE HAND, ONE HEART

CLARINET IN B♭

Lyrics by STEPHEN SONDHEIM
Music by LEONARD BERNSTEIN

8 SOMETHING'S COMING

CLARINET IN B♭

Lyrics by STEPHEN SONDHEIM
Music by LEONARD BERNSTEIN

2.
f
mf
To Coda
2
mf
D.S. al Coda
CODA
p
mp

9 SOMEWHERE

CLARINET IN B♭

Lyrics by STEPHEN SONDHEIM
Music by LEONARD BERNSTEIN

10 TONIGHT

CLARINET IN B♭

Lyrics by STEPHEN SONDHEIM
Music by LEONARD BERNSTEIN